TO:

_____

FROM:

_____

BUDDHISM FOR YOU

Prayer

BUDDHISM FOR YOU

Prayer

DAISAKU IKEDA

MIDDLEWAY
PRESS

Published by Middleway Press
A division of the SGI-USA
606 Wilshire Blvd., Santa Monica, CA 90401

© 2006 Soka Gakkai

Design by Lightbourne, Inc.

10 9 8 7 6 5 4 3

Library of Congress Cataloging-in-Publication Data

Ikeda, Daisaku.
    Buddhism for you. Prayer / Daisaku Ikeda.
        p. cm.

    ISBN-13: 978-0-9723267-9-7 (hardcover : alk. paper)
    I. Religious life--Soka Gakkai. 2. Prayer--Religious aspects--
Buddhism. I. Title.
BQ8499.I384B833 2006
294.3'5696--dc22

                                2006028526

ISBN: 978-0-9723267-9-7

Compassion is the very soul of Buddhism.
To pray for others, making their
problems and anguish our own;
to embrace those who are suffering,
becoming their greatest ally;
to continue giving them our support
and encouragement until they become
truly happy—it is in such humanistic actions
that Nichiren Buddhism
lives and breathes.

Prayer is not a feeble consolation;
it is a powerful, unyielding conviction.

✳

Prayer is the courage to persevere.
It is the struggle to overcome our own
weakness and lack of confidence in ourselves.
It is the act of impressing in the very depths
of our being the conviction that we can
change the situation without fail.

When we pray, we embrace the universe
with our lives and our determinations.

✳

Wisdom arises from prayer.
Prayer gives birth to confidence and joy.

✳

Prayer is not of the realm of logic or intellect.
It transcends these.

Ａfter we pray for something,
we need to struggle with all
our might to actualize it.
This is true faith.

❋

Ｂe diligent in developing your faith
until the last moment of your life.
Otherwise you will have regrets.

—*Nichiren*

Heb 11:1-3 - Faith is the confidence that what
we hope for will actually happen; it gives us
assurance about things we cannot see. Through
their faith the people in days of old earned a
good reputation. By faith we understand that
the entire universe was formed at God's
command, that we now see did not come
from anything that can be seen.

It is important to become people who view things not in terms of tiny, selfish concerns but from a larger, more generous perspective.
We have to pray to become more broad-minded and tolerant.

11:6 - It is impossible to please God w/out faith. Anyone who wants to come to Him must believe that God exists and that He rewards those who sincerely seek Him.

There is a marvelous Buddhist principle
that teaches that the living,
through their prayers and actions,
can pass on to their deceased friends
and loved ones the benefit
of the good causes
they have accumulated.

✳

Prayer functions like the sun.
It serves as the light that illuminates
the darkness of suffering.

*T*hose of you who have problems or sufferings, pray earnestly! Buddhism is a deadly serious win or lose struggle.

—*Josei Toda*

✳

*T*he religious spirit is a kind of mental capacity that turns nihilism into a bright future and despair into hope.

7

There may be times when you grow
impatient and anxious because it seems
like your prayers will never be answered.
But all prayers that lead to your happiness
will definitely be fulfilled. There is
absolutely no mistake about this.

✳

By praying, we can cleanse our lives
of negativity and illusions.
We can push everything
in the direction of happiness.

There are two kinds of benefits
from our prayers, those that are
immediately apparent, or conspicuous,
and those that we cannot see right away,
or inconspicuous. Inconspicuous benefit
is the focus of Nichiren Buddhism,
for it is what brings real happiness.

We have to make a
determination, pray and take action.
Unless we do so, our environment
will not change in the least.

✳

I am devoted to none but Truth
and I owe no discipline
to anybody but Truth.

—*Mahatma Gandhi*

The purpose of Nichiren Buddhism
is to enable us to realize victory in life.
The fact that our prayers are answered
is proof of the correctness of this teaching.

❋

Prayer in Buddhism deepens and expands
our common sense regarding the affairs of
daily life and the world. It reveals the
Law of life that we need to follow
in order to become happy.

Religion is proof of our humanity.
Of all the animals, only human beings
have the capacity for prayer, a most
solemn and sublime act.

✳

The most important thing
is to build an indestructible
palace of happiness
within our lives.

From the moment we begin to pray,
things start moving. The darker the night,
the closer the dawn. From the moment we chant
Nam-myoho-renge-kyo with a deep and powerful
resolve, the sun begins to rise in our hearts.
Hope—prayer is the sun of hope.

Become the happiest you can be
based upon your profound
and strong prayer.

Sometimes our prayers
are realized immediately
and sometimes they aren't.
When we look back later, however,
we can say with absolute conviction
that everything turned out
for the best.

There is no set form
or pattern for how we should pray.
Buddhism emphasizes being natural.
Therefore, simply pray earnestly,
without pretense, just as you are.

Buddhist prayer is a ceremony in which
our lives commune with the universe.
When we pray, we vigorously infuse the
microcosm of our individual existence
with the life force of the macrocosm,
of the entire universe.

Just as a morning walk or jog
may be pleasantly exhilarating
for both the body and the mind,
please chant Nam-myoho-renge-kyo
in a way that is personally satisfying to you—
one that leaves you feeling refreshed and
uplifted both mentally and physically.

Human beings have an undeniable instinct
for prayer. Religion first came into being
in response to this. Prayer did not come
into existence because of religion;
it was the other way around.

When we pray with appreciation
immense vitality wells forth.
From the depths of our lives,
we tap the wisdom to encourage others.
And our conduct translates into
value-creating activities perfectly responding
to the needs of our circumstances
and of those around us.

✳

In Nichiren Buddhism, it is said that
no prayer goes unanswered. But this is
very different from having every wish
instantly granted as if by magic.
All your prayers serve to propel you
in the direction of happiness.

Life is a struggle with ourselves.
It is a tug of war between
moving forward and regressing,
between happiness and unhappiness.
Those short on willpower or self motivation
should chant Nam-myoho-renge-kyo with
conviction to become people of strong will,
who can tackle any problem with real
seriousness and determination.

Buddhism teaches that the same power which
moves the universe exists within our lives.
Each individual has immense potential,
and a great change in the inner dimension
of one individual's life has the power
to touch the lives of others
and transform society.

✳

What are we praying for? How are we praying?
A person's state of life is expressed in his or her
prayer. Become people who pray with a broad
and deep resolve. Those who pray in this way
will amass tremendous good fortune.

Genuine faith is a sword of belief
and conviction that cuts through all suffering.
It is a bright light of hope that illuminates
the darkness and confusion.

A sense of responsibility
arises from prayer and action,
which in turn further deepen
our sense of responsibility.

Though one might point at the earth and miss it,
though one might bind up the sky,
though the tides might cease to ebb and flow
and the sun rise in the west, it could never
come about that the prayers of the
practitioner of the Lotus Sutra
would go unanswered.

—*Nichiren*

❋

Nam-myoho-renge-kyo
is the wellspring of the universe
and the fundamental power of life.
It is the ultimate expression of wisdom
and the foundation of all laws and principles.

Meditation for its own sake is absurd.
Shakyamuni clearly explains that true meditation
is not solitary contemplation beneath a tree
but playing an active role in society
while embracing the truth.

✳

Since the thoughts or ideas
that come to mind as we chant
Nam-myoho-renge-kyo represent
issues that concern us at that moment,
we should not consider them extraneous.
Instead, we should pray earnestly
about each one, whatever it may be.

Nevertheless, even though you chant
and believe in Myoho-renge-kyo,
if you think the Law is outside yourself,
you are embracing not the Mystic Law
but an inferior teaching.

—*Nichiren*

Just as a soft voice can be transformed
into a booming voice through
the use of a good megaphone,
when we chant Nam-myoho-renge-kyo
with heartfelt prayer, we can
move the entire universe.

Through intense prayer, we can
significantly transform our destiny,
as well as the destiny of our families and society.
It is vital to pray with resolute conviction.
Prayer stimulates wisdom
and fills us with life force.

Those who are most strongly
resolved to win will
definitely do so in the end.
The power that fuels
this resolve is prayer;
it is our faith.

We practice Buddhism
to make our prayers and dreams
come true and to achieve
the greatest possible happiness.

✳

Prayer is a struggle to expand our lives.

Because Buddhism entails practice,
tenacious efforts are required,
but these are all for your own sake.
If you want to have great benefits
or to develop a profound state of life,
you should exert yourself accordingly.

✳

Prayer in Nichiren Buddhism
is not something with which to merely
console ourselves in the face of hardships
or a diversion from worries; it helps us
create genuine fulfillment from our
innermost core and bring about
concrete positive results
in our daily lives.

Even if your prayer doesn't produce
concrete results immediately,
your continual prayer will
at some time manifest itself
in a form greater than you
had ever hoped.

By chanting Nam-myoho-renge-kyo,
we humbly praise the Buddha,
which means we are automatically
praising and reinforcing to the utmost
our own Buddhahood.

No matter how earnestly
Nichiren prays for you,
if you lack faith, it will be like
trying to set fire to wet tinder.
Spur yourself to muster
the power of faith.

—*Nichiren*

We need a higher sense of purpose,
and when we have a higher sense of purpose,
our prayers about personal matters
are more easily answered.

Wisdom emerges through prayer.
Victory emerges through wisdom.

What was Shakyamuni Buddha's
most ardent prayer? It was for
all people to become happy.

The struggle we go through to have
our prayers answered makes us stronger.
If we were to immediately get
everything we prayed for, we would
become spoiled and decadent.
We would lead indolent lives,
devoid of any hard work or struggle.
As a result, we would become
shallow human beings. What, then,
would be the point of faith?

There are no rules governing
how we should pray.
There's no need to be
something we aren't.

✳

Buddhism is reason.
Our prayers cannot be answered
if we fail to make efforts
appropriate to our situation.

One thing is certain: That is that
the power of belief, the power of thought,
will move reality in the direction of
what we believe and conceive of it.
If you really believe you can
do something, you can.
That is a fact.

❋

Prayers are invisible,
but if we pray steadfastly, they will
definitely effect clear results in our lives
and surroundings over time.

Compose your life patiently
with the power of faith.
Direct your efforts into this channel.
Once you realize that complaining is useless,
you can chant Nam-myoho-renge-kyo in earnest.

—*Josei Toda*

❋

There are many elements involved
in a prayer being answered,
but the important thing
is to keep praying until it is.

When you bring forth your Buddhahood
by chanting Nam-myoho-renge-kyo,
your passionate nature will become
your impetus for progress,
a strong sense of justice
and a burning desire
to help other people.

＊

The true spirit of meditation lies in
manifesting our innate wisdom in society
and resolutely struggling for the happiness
of ourselves and others, and to
construct a better society.

May all beings be happy!
Whether he stands, walks, sits or lies down,
as long as he is awake, he should develop
this mindfulness. This they say
is the noblest living here.

—*Shakyamuni*

When a stalemate arises
we must first pray,
then take action.

As human beings, let us
reach beyond our small, limited selves
and attain an all-encompassing state of being,
our hearts communing with the vast universe.

*

There's no limit
to how many things we can pray about.
It just means that the more desires we have,
the more sincere and abundant
our prayer will be.

To pray, ponder and move
for the sake of people's happiness
is to awaken real sincerity.

❋

Prayer is the key. The important thing
is to pray with steadfast determination.
There is nothing more powerful than prayer.
This is not mere theory. Without prayer,
all our efforts will ultimately
get us nowhere.

❋

Prayer becomes manifest in action,
and action has to be backed up by prayer.

Buddhism is not a religion that
closes its eyes to people's suffering;
it is a teaching that opens people's eyes.
To turn away our eyes from the contradictions
of society and rid ourselves of all worldly thoughts
is not the way of Buddhist practice.

❉

A coward cannot have
any of his prayers answered.

—*Nichiren*

The power of prayer
is the decisive means for overcoming
periods of stagnation or difficulty.

By continuing to pray, you can reflect
on yourself with unflinching honesty
and begin to move your life
in a positive direction on the path
of earnest, steady effort.

Buddhism means putting the teachings
into practice. Practice equals faith.
With sincere prayer and action, our desires
cannot possibly fail to be fulfilled.

Earnestly pray and take action each day,
encouraging people at every opportunity.
It is important to encourage those we
come in contact with, even with
just a single word or phrase.

*T*hose who chant Myoho-renge-kyo
[the title of the Lotus Sutra] even without
understanding its meaning realize
not only the heart of the Lotus Sutra,
but also the "main cord," or
essential principle of the Buddha's
lifetime teaching.

–Nichiren

To pray each time we face a problem,
overcoming it and elevating our
life-condition as a result—this is the path of
"changing earthly desires into enlightenment"
taught in Nichiren Buddhism.

Faith is not dependent on
ceremonies and formalities.
It is a struggle to transform
our very being.

It is our efforts to pray for and
help another person to become happy
that represent the foremost popular movement
and that directly contribute to the creation
of a truly democratic society.

To offer prayers
is to conduct a dialogue,
an exchange, with the universe.

Therefore, we know that the prayers offered
by a practitioner of the Lotus Sutra
will be answered just as
an echo answers a sound.

—*Nichiren*

For people who embrace
Nam-myoho-renge-kyo,
to worry about friends and pray for
their happiness comes naturally.
We should not forget just how noble
such efforts are.

How, then, can we come to perceive
that there is no difference between
our minds and the Buddha's mind?
Only through our human powers
of faith and practice.

❋

A person of deep prayer
is never deadlocked.

Buddhism aims to make people free
in the most profound sense;
its purpose is not to restrict or constrain.
Chanting Nam-myoho-renge-kyo
is a right, not an obligation.

It's natural for prayers to center on
your own desires and dreams.
There's no need to pretend that you're
praying for something lofty when you're not.
By praying naturally, without affectation
or reservation, for what you seek most of all,
you'll gradually come to develop a higher
and more expansive life-condition.

Compassion is the very soul of Buddhism.
To pray for others, making their
problems and anguish our own;
to embrace those who are suffering,
becoming their greatest ally;
to continue giving them our support
and encouragement until they become
truly happy—it is in such humanistic actions
that Nichiren Buddhism
lives and breathes.

You must practice faith with
abundant gratitude, deeply appreciative
of even the slightest improvement!
—*Josei Toda*

In this egoistic world, to offer prayers and
work hard for the happiness of others,
as well as for oneself,
is magnificent.

Amid this harsh reality,
people yearn from the depths of
their beings to live with dignity
and for their lives to have meaning,
and they make efforts toward that end.
The product of these human yearnings,
these prayers, is religion.
Religion was born
from prayer.

It's important to remember that
your prayers always reflect your state of life.
In that respect, prayer is a solemn means
to raise your life-condition.
And to get exactly the results
that you're praying for,
it is crucial to make determined,
single-minded efforts
toward that goal.

When we hear of a friend
struggling somewhere, or that
those in some other region or community
are in difficulty or facing a daunting challenge,
we send them our prayers as earnestly as if
praying for our own happiness.

Now, if you wish to attain Buddhahood,
you have only to lower the banner
of your arrogance, cast aside the staff
of your anger, and devote yourself
exclusively to the one vehicle
of the Lotus Sutra.

—*Nichiren*

A person of faith seeks self-mastery;
a person of ambition or power
seeks to control others. A person of faith
takes action, works hard and struggles to
overcome his or her inner weakness;
a person driven by a desire
for power forces others to work
for his own selfish purpose,
never reflecting upon himself.

When we are aware that
each moment of each day,
each gesture and step we take is
truly mystical and full of wonder,
we will live our lives with
greater thought and care.

The highest offering to the Buddha
is not to worship something
reminiscent of the Buddha.
Rather, it is to inherit
the Buddha's spirit.

Who answers our prayers?
We do—through faith and effort.
No one does it for us.

*Additional books in this series
are available and include:*

Courage
Determination
Love

To order please visit:
www.MiddlewayPress.com

*For more information about the SGI,
please visit:* www.sgi-usa.org